JOHS. B. THUE

INTO THE FJORDS

from Bergen to Sogn

SKALD 2007

Photos: Idun Husabø Anderssen 100, Oskar Andersen 83, 102, 103, Leiv
Bergum 34, 47, 51, 54, 56, 64b, 72, 93, 106a, Guttorm Flatabø 58, 111, Fylkes-
arkivet 44, Magne Hamre 32, 37, 38a, Trond J. Hansen 69, 70, Petri Henriks-
son 10, 11, 80, Lars Nes 38b, 52, 57, 60, 77, 106b, Norsk Bremuseum 73, OSY
41, 64a, 67, 84, 85, 109, Bjørn Skanke Sande 49, 62, 68, Simone Stibbe 79,
Robin Strand 4, 6, 8, 9, 12, 15, 16, 17, 18, 22, 23, 25, 27, 28, 30, 48, 61, 74, 86,
87, 94, 97, 98, 104, Helge Sunde 59, 88, 91, 96, Utlån Johs. B. Thue 20, Utlån
Mulla Kvikne 43.

Cover photos: Leiv Bergum (front), Robin Strand (a),
Trond J. Hansen (b), Lars Nes (c)

English translation: Jan Talsethagen

Graphic design: Silje Nes
Print: Kaunas

© SKALD AS 2007

Telephone: + 47 57 65 41 55
e-mail: forlag@skald.no
www.skald.no

ISBN 978-82-7959-102-3 (norsk utgåve)
ISBN 978-82-7959-103-0 (English edition)

CONTENTS

PREFACE

Once again I am back in Bergen. In this city I have studied and worked. Out to learn, home to earn, was the idea. My children were born there. In their childhood years they tinged their words with the characteristic Bergen dialect so different from the neighbouring dialects. Then we moved back to my roots in Sogn. They quickly took to the Sogn dialect and became true *Sognings* and rural people, as did my grandchildren a generation later.

As a child I often played with children of my own age from Bergen. In the summertime they came with their grandparents and parents to Balestrand, my home village. Red and white residences, country houses along the shore. We played the same games. In the white-painted *Sogne* rowboat we sat on the same thwart, using a hand-held fishing line with a lead sinker. Blue mussels were used as bait. We caught the whiting – the chicken of the fjord – the staple summer fare in the summer residences. Bergen has always been close to my heart.

I majored in history at the university. It goes without saying that my love for history will tinge my words as well. My senses observe, rooted in my educational background and sphere of interest. Besides, any encounter with city and landscape is bound to be a subjective experience. Other people's experiences will never be the same as mine.

People from Bergen love their city. There is no proper Christmas holiday season unless there are four or five new books about Bergen under the Christmas tree. People love to read about themselves and their city. Come to think of it, so do people from Sogn. In this way they get a theoretical foundation to what they see and observe in their everyday lives.

Recently I have enjoyed reading some books about Bergen that have provided me with inspiring and informative material for this book. These books are "Bergtatt av Bergen" by Espen Børhaug and Frank Johnsen, "Slik ble vi bergensere" by Agnete Nesse, "Bergenske kvinner" by Elisabeth Aasen, and above all the outstanding "Steinbyen Bergen", written by Tom Heldal and Øystein J. Jansen.

The main foundation of this travel handbook, however, is naturally my general knowledge of urban and regional history.

⊲ *Idyllic street scene from Nordnes.*

Nordnes, Bergen.

BERGEN – A JOURNEY TO A DIFFERENT WORLD

I am standing at the Fish Market in Bergen. Behind me the hills are painted in brown and red on this snowless winter's day. Around me at an arm's length is the City. I am watching the bustling city life, the streets and houses, the docks, and the monumental buildings. This is Bergen, our city and centre, too, the only city for the people from Sogn. It is the marketplace for the city but also for the regions, the meeting-place for people from western and northern Norway for centuries, dating all the way back to the 11th century.

The centre of the city of Bergen has changed considerably. A century ago, 90,000 persons lived there. At present, the number has been drastically reduced to 30,000, which, by the way corresponds to the population of the whole Sogn region. Due to urban sprawl, Bergen has changed the old fishing and agricultural villages in the surrounding areas. The population of the city municipality is approaching 250,000. This development is not caused by the virility of Bergen men and women. The birth rate follows a downward trend, but every year the net movement of people from other parts of the country shows a surplus of some 800 people. For centuries, Bergen has used wet nurses from the villages of western Norway.

"The City fjord", people from northern Norway called these waters, the fjords and the straits north of Bergen, as they came sailing in their *jakts* heavily

Behind the Hanseatic docks we are taken back to bygone days.

⊰ *The Fløibanen Funicular is one of Bergen's most famous and popular tourist attractions.*

The Bergen bakers have been strongly influenced by German baking traditions.

laden with stockfish. People from Sogn transported their firewood in smaller *jekts*. The City fjord stretched from Alden all the way south to Vågsbotnen. The island of Alden rises from the ocean west of Askvoll in Sunnfjord. This island, which was frequently referred to as "The Norwegian Horse", marked the first sighting of land for sailors coming in from the ocean.

MORE THAN A MARKET PLACE

The Marketplace in Bergen is more than an ordinary market. Here we can get a whiff of European air. The local bakeries are of German origin, and the bread and pastries have a German flavour and sometimes even German names. The bakery products spread towards coast and fjord. The white-clothed baker lit his ovens before the crack of dawn, kneading the dough to make langebrød (literally: long loaves of bread), cinnamon rolls, Wittenberg loaves, and various pastries. His apprenticeship was served in Bergen, of course. He represented the new times. The long loaves of bread were kneaded with a mixture of rye flour and wheat. Rye was imported from the plains along the Black Sea. Ships from Bergen anchored up in the port of Odessa. Of all Bergen industries, shipping was perhaps the most important, and, for this reason Bergen has its own Maritime Museum, located among university buildings.

Rye had been cultivated by Germanic, Celtic and Slav peoples for more than 2500 years. Our marginal climate made it hard to cultivate rye so we stuck to oats and barley. In the village of Kvamsøy, blessed with a sunny climate, we find the place name "Ruggjerdet" (literally: the rye field). Sogn was divided into oats and barley areas. The oats villages belonged to the coastal areas. A common feature in all the Sogn villages – with the exception of Hafslo – was a shortage of grain. In the 19th century, therefore, a comprehensive network of bartering was established between coastal and fjord villages; fish was exchanged for potatoes. Between the fjord villages and Bergen; firewood for grain.

When the wind blows easterly from land, from the water reservoir up at Svartediket and Årstad out towards the Vågen, we can vaguely sense the sweet smell of malt in the smoke from the chimneys of the Hansa Brewery. The brand name of Hansa is a household name in western Norway. To hansa means to go

The market place at the head of the bay of Vågen has served as the soul of Bergen for centuries.

Dutch in terms of beverages. The old jekt skippers from Sogn brought home Dutch genever (gin), and together with home-brewed malt beer, smoked salmon and flatbread this made for a feast. People from Sogn were sceptical to brandy and other darkly coloured spirits up to the 1890s. Through the port of Bergen European culture entered many a living room in Sogn.

In some places in Sogn the word for "Wednesday" used to be merkredag

or mekran derived from the French word mercredi, of course. However, the cultural impulses could go the other way as well. The cultural struggle between Sogn and Bergen could be fought in most arenas, including the Christmas Eve fare. For a long while, the tradition with lutefisk (cod steeped in a lye solution) based on stockfish brought home from Bergen, served with yellow mushy peas, bacon and flatbread, held its position against the crofters' fare

The theatre "Den Nationale Scene" opened in 1876.

of pinnakjøtt (salted and dried ribs of mutton or lamb). Then the lutefisk lost its position on the home front and was relegated to restaurant menus in the pre-Christmas season. The rustic dish of pinnakjøtt, served with mealy potatoes and mashed swedes now spreads its delicious smell in city streets, suburbs and quiet hamlets. The village won the battle against the city with regards to the Christmas Eve fare.

In former times, fish was traded directly from the docked fishing vessels. Fish from the fjords, the bays and the ocean was weighed on board with a pair of scales which frequently left room for some bargaining both in terms of quality and price. When the deal was done, the fish was thrown up to the buyers on the quayside. A true Bergen citizen looked upon the act of buying fish as an art form, comparable to a theatre performance at Den Nationale

Scene, the country's first theatre. The Bergen dialect with its characteristic uvular 'r' actually became the first national stage language, used by the prima donna Johanne Dybwad. Henrik Ibsen and Bjørnstjerne Bjørnson were both theatre managers there and both married strong Bergen women: Suzanne Thoresen and Karoline Reimers respectively. Bergen was the country's intellectual capital around 1850. The Bergen merchant families took a leading part in the cultural awakening which goes under the name of the "Norwegianism" movement. Names such as Krohn, Beyer, Giertsen, Konow, Prahl and Bull were the first western adherents of the new language movement. At that time, people from Sogn were fast asleep intellectually and culturally.

FRUIT FROM OCEAN AND FJORD

Between January and April the market stallholders seek shelter in a big tent. However, the rest of the year trading takes place from stalls in the open. At the fruit market we find an abundance of delicious Norwegian apple varieties such as Gravenstein, Åkerø, Summerred, and Aroma. And what have we observed there? Yes, the following hand-written stall notice: "Aroma from Sogn picked on a moonlit night on 15 September, 2002". The stallholders obviously know their trade and they have turned selling almost into an art form. Some stallholders have got hold of small quantities of the new pear varieties called Fridtjof and Ingeborg, but the dominant varieties are still Amanlis, Philip, and Grev Moltke. The Bergen hinterland – Sogn and Hardanger in particular – undoubtedly produces the tastiest fruit in northern Europe. Even if these regions have a marginal climate for growing fruit, the long summer days bless the fruit with a highly aromatic flavour. The days can be long in Sogn.

The top quality of Norwegian fruit is the result of a long process of research and development. The basis, however, has always been the older and climatically adapted apple and pear varieties. Today profitability is very low and orchards are mowed down with chain saws. The whole culture of fruit growing is disappearing. Thus, the Aroma picked in moonshine in mid-September may soon become history. And what about the Fish Market itself, the very life and soul of Bergen, one of the country's major attractions? It seems as if the Bergen citizens themselves have abandoned the Fish Market as a place to buy fish pro-

Salmon from coastal waters and fjords is an important and popular commodity in Bergen – sold fresh or cured.

Bergen is the country's undisputed rain city with more than 230 days of rainy weather every year.

ducts. Fresh fish is hard to find. Now the main products are rolls with smoked salmon, souvenirs of various categories and qualities, colourful T-shirts, all watering down the essence and smell of Bergen. People rush by, on their way to the Fløybanen funicular, carrying 1.1 million passengers every year.

THE JEKT SHIPPING ROUTES

This story illustrates how the important jekt routes functioned. The jekts linked Sogn to the market in Bergen, dating back to the Middle Ages. The

jekts were square-sail-rigged vessels, depending completely on catching the wind from behind. Consequently, the skippers needed an easterly wind to get out of the bay in Bergen, but had to rely on a westerly wind to take them home into the Sognefjord. The fair wind from the west was called Sogna-bør which also brought rain and plankton into the fjord. Beliefs and magic superstitions frequently deal with ways of mastering and pleasing the forces of nature. People truly believed that Finns were able to master the forces of nature and knew more than most people. One common belief was that it was possible to "bribe the wind". "Sailing porridge", covered with heaps of butter, could lead to more wind. Another belief was to put shilling coins into cracks on the mast. They never prayed for God's help to get wind. In spite of these magical remedies, the Bergen expeditions could take weeks, even months. Up until the late 19th century it was said that a return voyage to Bergen could take as long as a sow's gestation period, lasting three months, three weeks, three days and three hours.

FIREWOOD FOR THE CITY AND CITY COMMODITIES

The most important commodity from the central villages of Sogn was always firewood. "Firewood for the city", it was called. Burning firewood at home that was meant to be sold in Bergen was unheard of, and even considered shameful. This was almost equal to burning paper money. Split, two-feet-long pieces of firewood from birch were always piled in cords, an old measure unit of about two ells (six feet) in length and height. When metric measures were introduced in 1876, the length of the split piece of firewood still remained 60 centimetres (two feet), but the cord was now two metres long and two metres high. The firewood was stacked on the docks of Bergen, carefully supervised by official controllers with black caps and stamp and who smelled of liquor. Lavik – the important ferry port in the Sognefjord – has got its name from

The square-rigged "jekts" were heavily laden with firewood.

THE OLD CONNECTION

Bergen, then, was our city, the old city for people from Sogn. There we should behave like proper city people, not dress in clothes made of frieze, and not smell of cowshed and acrid silage. My mother was firmly reminded by her grandfather when she went to Bergen to attend the first "New-Norwegian" trade school in the country that she should not "stare into all the windows". There they were also introduced to new mythical forces. The local wood nymph had to give way. The folklore collector Sjur Bøyum has recorded a typical wandering story: Helge Lidal from the Fjærlandsfjord once lay wind-bound with his jekt in Bergen. He had sold his load of firewood, butter, and cheese, and had bought commodities such as grain, salt, and an anker (small barrel) of genever (Dutch gin) to cure rheumatism. However, lack of wind prevented him from leaving the bay. Then it struck him that he had seen a Finn further up in the city. It was commonly known that Finns had knowledge of many a thing, including how to cause favourable wind. He found the Finn, and the latter was willing to help him out.

– I must have something in return for helping you, though, said the Finn. I would like a leg of cured mutton.

Helge then gave him the choicest leg of mutton he could find.

– As you were so generous as to give me your best leg of mutton, I shall give you more than enough wind for your homeward voyage, said the Finn.

Standing on his left leg, he tied three knots on a red handkerchief that he was holding behind his back.

– When you untie the first knot, this will give you fair wind. The second knot will give you howling wind, but the third knot must not be touched at all because then a dreadful storm will be unleashed, he said, shaking Helge's hand.

Helge returned to his jekt and made everything ready for his voyage home. He then grabbed the tiller with one hand and untied the first knot with the other. No sooner had he done this, he suddenly felt a breeze, starting up at the mountain of Ulriken, and then it came dancing down the mountainside, out past Stadsporten (the city gate) and across the bay of Vågen. Helge cast off, sailed past the currents of Straumane, and soon reached Rutletangane. Then he opened the second knot. The jekt made good headway into the Sognefjord itself, rushing past Nordeide and Måren. He caught a glimpse of the point of Koldingsnes at the entrance to the Lånefjord. There he was tempted to touch the third knot, but in the wink of an eye a howling westerly storm was raging on the fjord. Filled with fear, Helge lost no time in tightening the knot again.

the word lad (pile of cut wood). There people piled their firewood down by the sea. It was not without reason that Ole Elias Holck – the Eidsvoll Assembly representative from 1814 whose statue can be seen at Alværa – in his "Description of Lavik" writes that the sale of firewood to Bergen was always by far the most important source of income for people in the parish of Lavik.

The old buildings of St. Jørgens Hospital are today used as a Leprosy Museum.

⊳ *"Bryggen" was called "Tyskebryggen" (the German Docks) until 1945.*

When the times were hard, much firewood was cut for the Bergen market. Up until about 1860, two shipments of firewood were sent every year.

The purpose of the farmers' autumn expedition to Bergen was to sell their produce – mostly butter and cheese – from the summer's toil on the mountain farms. A speciality from Sogn was gamalost (literally: old cheese). The farmers returned from Bergen with various commodities such as salt and other groceries, iron, and grain. It was especially important to get hold of salt before the slaughtering season started. Both along the coast and inland it was common to economize with the salt. A lot of fish, therefore, was raka (fermented), a preservation method without too much use of salt. Fermented herring ("sour herring") was one of most appreciated dishes for people from western and northern Norway. This preservation method died out, however, when superstition led people to believe that eating fermented fish could cause leprosy. The lepers at the St. Jørgen's Hospital in Bergen smelled of fermented herring. This hospital – also known as Spitalen – is the oldest foundation in the country. The modern hospital town of Bergen originated in the monasticism of the late Middle Ages. When the Reformation put an end to Catholic faith and church art in 1536, the St. Jørgen's Hospital took over the entire Selje manor that many farmers in Sogn paid an annual land tax to. For this reason, every year butter and gamalost were sent to the hospital which later owned the Harastølen tuberculosis sanatorium in Luster, once the mountain farm of the Fuhr farm.

NATIONAL CAPITAL

Bergen was originally called Bjorgyn or Bjørgvin. This may signify the pasture or the field between sea and mountains. Further inland was the king's manor at Alrekstadir, today called Årstad. The harbour at Vågen was free of ice, and the water was calm, sheltered by the seven mountains surrounding Bergen. The Bjørgvin name was later latinized to Bergae, and then changed slightly to the present Bergen. Other explanations of the Bergen name have been put forward, usually by referring to Germanic roots. In the early 20th century the name Bjørgvin once more turned up as a national language

At Nordnes we can still come across old and well-preserved buildings.

dream, caused by a linguistic movement all over the country. Cities should revert to their Old Norse names. Only one successful change was made when the nation's capital Kristiania got back its old name Oslo. Bjørgvin did not catch on as a name for Bergen, but the term is used for the diocese.

A number of historians still think that we have yet to find the answer to how Bergen actually developed. In the official history book of Bergen, writ-

ten by the eminent medieval expert Knut Helle, the conclusion is that it is a fair assumption that Bergen can be categorized among those cities that simply developed on their own accord. There may have been a built-up area of a couple of hundred inhabitants at Vågen before Olav Kyrre's realm from 1066 to 1093. Olav Kyrre was the peace-loving king whose name is indelibly linked to the very founding of the city of Bergen.

SOGN IN BERGEN

Bergen is now a significant cultural city. Cultural production has become an important industry, all year round. We can go to concerts in Håkonshallen, our national Babylon, destroyed so many times. The architect from Lærdal, Johan Lindstrøm, restored the Hall that was reopened in 1961. You can stroll along the small lake of Lille Lungegårdsvann in the centre of Bergen. On its western side the Bergen Art Museum is located, where so much of the artist Knut Rumohr's magnificent work is on display, depicting the people and countryside of Frønningen in the Sognefjord. The architect and building manager Peter Blix's restoration work can be seen many places, both in Håkonshallen and Domkirken (the Cathedral). Blix is also renowned for his protection and restoration work in connection with churches in Sogn, in particular with the Hove stone church at Vik. In addition, he designed Hotel Mundal at Fjærland. Blix used soapstone as a building material, quarried at Dale in Arnafjord, also in the restored Cathedral. Johan is not the only Lindstrøm who has made a name for himself. This name is also well known in the school history of Bergen. Sophie Lindstrøm (1849–1942) also came from Lærdal. At home they had governesses from Bergen as was the case for Knut Rumohr at Frønningen a few decades later. In 1881, she established Sophie Lindstrøm's School for Girls and became known as a school reformer. She was an outdoor person. On their way to Rundemannen, one of the seven mountains encircling Bergen, people could meet the then 80-year-old woman, "wearing long black skirts, a black hat with ostrich feathers and black gloves".

In the early 12th century, Bjørgvin emerges as a royal capital, later on also a cathedral city, when the see was moved from Selje. The judicial authority was moved from Gulen, the old Gulatinget. The centralization of power and administration has a 900-year-long history in our country. At the same time, Bergen was beginning to attract both national and foreign tradesmen. The Munkeliv Kloster monastery was established at Nordnes in the early 12th century. From the Marketplace the direct view of Nordnes is blocked by the high buildings along the Strand docks, but we can discern the outline of a hill and a protruding point on the left-hand side when facing westwards towards the harbour and the sea. The king himself put the millstone quarries in Åfjorden in Hyllestad at the disposal of the Benedictine monastery of Munkeliv at Nordnes to provide it with an economic foundation. The millstones from Hyllestad were exported to Denmark and northern Europe as early as the 8th century. At Nordnes today we find the Bergen Aquarium with 300,000 visitors every year, and above all, the Institute of Marine Research with a staff of

> *The Bergen Art Museum is located by the lake of Lille Lungegårdsvann.*

"Gamle Bergen" (Old Bergen) is a unique collection of old and picturesque wooden houses.

some 600, enjoying a high international reputation in marine research.

The city of Bergen had an early westerly orientation through trade and shipping, not least towards Britain and the other islands to the west. The stockfish, fished, processed and transported to the storage houses along the inner docks of Vågen by the northern Norwegians may partly explain the growth of the city. During Lent stockfish was perhaps the product most in demand throughout Catholic Europe. The ships returned home to Norway with

grain and wine. In the 14th century, Germans came to Bergen. These were trade administrators for the Hanseatic League's headquarters in Lübeck, Bremen, and Hamburg. In the course of a century they had established themselves in the city on a year-round basis, thereby driving Norwegian merchants and sailors out of business. In a relatively short time, they had full control of trade and transport. Up until the German capitulation after the Second World War, Bryggen was called Tyskebryggen (the German docks),

and I for one still use that term. Mariakirken (the Maria Church) was called Tyskekirken (the German Church) as late as 1945.

The capital of Norway may not have been moved to Oslo if Eirik Magnusson, the young king towards the end of the 13th century, had not fallen down from a horse and suffered an early death. His brother, Håkon V. Magnusson, never moved his administration at Akershus in Oslo back to Bergen. Nevertheless, up until the 1830s, Bergen had a higher population than Oslo. Bergen has lost to Oslo in terms of population and industry, as well as political power. This is a loss that stretches several centuries. The same trend has taken place in Sogn. No region in Norway has had a more negative population trend than the villages along the Sognefjord. But both Bergen and Sogn have had their revenge. In the great, critical moments in out history, a Bergen citizen always rose to the occasion as a national saviour: Wilhelm Frimann Koren Christie was President of the Norwegian Parliament in the freedom year of 1814. In 1905, when Norway broke loose from the union with Sweden, Christian Michelsen stood at the national helm. In the dramatic April days in 1940, Carl Hoachim Hambro emerged as a unifying person with all his authority and managerial skills. People from Bergen won elsewhere what they lost behind their own city walls. In retrospect, we may naturally ponder this question: What would our country look like if Bergen political shrewdness had been used to break the Oslo power, the centralized power, and instead build up a regional power?

ON MY WAY FROM BERGEN TO SOGN

I am still standing at the Marketplace in Bergen, facing the fjord, the real city fjord. I see boats coming and leaving the harbour. This harbour is definitely the biggest cruise terminal in the country. 200,000 cruise passengers visit this town every year. Bergen is the real fjord city, the entrance and the gateway to the fjords, our only international tourist destination. Whereas buses and planes are mere transport means, a voyage appeals to our innermost feelings. This is the way people have always travelled. The lake, the sea, the ocean, and the fjord are all "ready-made" arteries that need no political approval or decisions. Whenever you travel by boat, you feel you are at one with the basic natural elements. Spiritual harmony this is called. This is a state of mind we all yearn for.

From the Marketplace in Bergen, from the streets and buildings with so many traces and memories from my hamlets and villages, my thoughts wander to the Sognefjord with all its troughs, fjord branches, bays and straits. Sogn is the name of the winding landscape past currents, points and bays

◁ *"Bryggen" reveals old building techniques.*

Along the coast people have built their houses in sheltered coves in an open landscape.

along the Sognefjord. Furthest to the west the land dives into the ocean at Nåra. This is the archipelago of Solund that we can visit by taking the postal boat. There we find the idyllic setting of Gåsvær, and also the island of Utvær, an old lighthouse station and the westernmost point on the map of Norway.

Sogn – what does it actually mean? In fjords and river pools we can some-times witness a foamy surge or whirlpool (sog in Norwegian) that seems to want to take hold of you and hide you. The name of Sogn, then, is derived from this natural phenomenon where bottom water wells up and mixes with

surface water at the same time as surface water sinks down to the bottom. Where the warm Gulf Stream meets the southbound cold ocean currents in the Norwegian Sea, the conditions for generating this circulation are especially favourable. Huge whirlpool currents help to circulate bottom water up to the surface. This natural phenomenon that created foam probably led to the name Sogn. Aphrodite in Greek mythology was also born of sea-foam.

In former times this area along the entire Songefjord was called Sygnafylket and its people sygnir. The whole landscape became a separate tax

collection district during the union with Denmark, lasting well into the late 19ᵗʰ century. The tax collection district identity is fortunately still intact, safeguarding characteristics and institutions. In the south, migrant peoples put names to the landscape. Hordar came to what is now the county of Hordaland with place names such as Hordvik, Hordabø, and Hordnes. Ryger came to the present county of Rogaland. Sygnir (people from Sogn), on the other hand, seems to have been named after a natural phenomenon linked to the whirling fjord. We did not take land; we were there from the very beginning.

The name of Sogn and its derived forms is widespread. We first come across it far out in the ocean west of Solund to describe underwater rocks licked by foaming waves. In the shipping lane north of Bergen there is a beacon on Sogneuksen. Sognesjøen is a wide stretch of fjord and ocean surrounded by place names containing the Sogn name in one form or another. A case in point is Sygnefest where the sygnir people settled down on the mainland. Due west of Sygnefest the point of Vardeneset juts into the sea. Varde means cairn, and fires were built at these cairns to warn neighbouring villages of impending unrest or war. Other place names are Sognnes and Sogneskollen.

When we cross the mountains over to the Gudbrandsdal valley we find the name again as an eastern extremity in the form of Sognefjellet. This mountain pass was called the Sognefjell road, not by people from Sogn, but by the inhabitants of the valleys to the east. This was the salt road towards the fjord and Sogn, where also people from the valleys of Valdres and Hallingdal got their salt of life. The road also became the eastern farmers' contact with Bergen. The Bergen merchants reached far with their commodities. The road across the Sognefjell Mountains is our national literary road. Henrik Wergeland, Henrik Ibsen, and Edvard Grieg to name but a few, travelled across this mountain pass, and this perilous journey left an indelible impression on them. The churchyard at Fortun provided Ibsen with the setting for the vicar's speech in his drama "Peer Gynt". The poet Wergeland who had his ancestral roots from the farm Werkland in Gulen was terrified by the wild forces of nature while travelling by boat on the Sognefjord. Some 175 years ago he described in vivid detail the fear and terror of praying travellers who dared to challenge the unpredictable wind conditions of the Sognefjord.

At the boundaries of Sogn, both north and south of the Sognefjord, we find names referring to the place. In Jølster we have Søgnesand, the gateway to the glacier road across to Fjærland. Far to the north, in the valley of Sunndalen in Nordfjord, the gap of Sogneskaret marks another road across to the valley of Jostedalen which was probably settled by people from Nordfjord

◁ *The coast along western Norway is extremely exposed to wind and waves.*

GULATINGET

At the entrance to the Sognefjord lies Gulen, where the judicial assembly Gulatinget convened from the period of King Harald Hårfagre (Fairhair) until about 1300 when the assembly was moved to Bergen. We can look upon the ting as a meeting-place between the farming communities of western Norway and the two public institutions of authority – king and church – which both sought to organize and get control of the country during the Middle Ages. Historians look upon the older Gulatingslov as a testimony of the conditions in the farming community and the roles played by king and church there. The older Gulatingslov is important, not only in a Norwegian perspective, but also in a Nordic and European context. It clearly demonstrates a farming community and its assembly representatives as extremely independent men. This independence concerns matters in such important areas as legislation, jurisdiction, as well as negotiations with king and church on issues of mutual interest.

and Gudbrandsdalen after the Black Death. Sogn is surrounded by place names showing that this is an ancient kingdom. Maybe the Icelandic accounts about king Bele contain a grain of historical truth where we can read the following: "This story starts with king Bele who ruled over the county of Sygnafylket". We, too, had our own king.

THE MILLSTONE COUNTRY

In the centre of the village of Hyllestad, competent enthusiasts, geologists and archaeologists are now developing a unique cultural heritage site. We have earlier referred to Bergen as the stone city. Hyllestad is the stone village, and we find traces of the Hyllestad stone in the centre of Bergen, for example in the stairs down to Steinkjelleren, where the exhibition of the legendary local artist Audun Hetland is on display. Walking along the river of Myklebustelva in Hyllestad – the old boundary between Sogn and Sunnfjord, north of the entrance to the Sognefjord – provides us with food for thought of ties far back in our history and ties out to Europe. We observe piles of stone chips and broken millstones, wreckage everywhere.

The millstones were the stones of life. They crushed the grain – "God's loan" – and ground flour. As early as in Deuteronomy we read that "No man shall take the nether or upper stone to pledge: for he taketh a man's life to pledge". We are on completely safe ground when we say that porridge and bread were the most important elements in the everyday diet throughout the Viking Age and the Middle Ages. In order to use the grain to make porridge, it was enough to crush

Hardbakke is the municipal centre of Solund.

the husk. To make bread, the grain needed to be finely ground. Handmills were found in every household, and it was considered women's work to use them. It is a safe assumption that the handmill was one of the central elements in the household, on a par with the fireplace and water source.

↖ *Utvær was the westernmost "skipsreie" (small administrative unit) in the country.*

↙ *Raw materials for millstones testify to an important export industry as early as the 12th century.*

The hills along the river of Myklebustelva, where the Millstone Park is now established and forms part of the cultural production in the county of Sogn og Fjordane, supplied a big market with millstones. This trade had been going on at least as far back as the 9th century when Norway was unified into one kingdom under the Sogning Harald Hårfagre (Fairhair). Thus we find traces of these Hyllestad stones on Iceland, in the south of Sweden, in Denmark, on the islands of Gotland and Bornholm, in Germany, and even as far away as to the forests, rivers, and corn fields east of the Baltic Sea. Once again we see proof of the important part played by Bergen in everything that had to do with European contact. Bergen was the logistics hub, a storage place, also for the export of millstones.

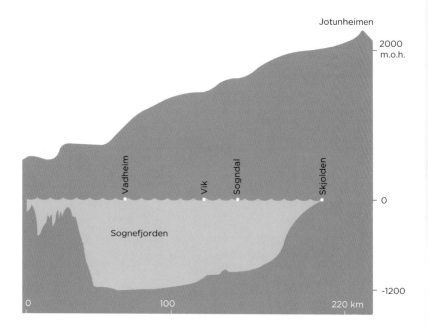

THE FJORD

A voyage on a fjord is a well-known trademark for the tourist nation Norway and a trump card in the marketing of tourism. The fjords of western and northern Norway represent a unique landscape that is hardly found anywhere else on the globe. Admittedly, there are fjords on Greenland and New Zealand, in Alaska and Chile, but what characterizes the Norwegian fjord landscape is its long history of settlement with its cultural landscape almost intact.

During a succession of ice ages, glacial erosion created the fjordscape as we see it today. The glaciers glided down the river valleys, transporting sediments that were deposited on the ocean floor. Then they started working on harder rock such as granite, gabbro and gneiss, eroding and breaking loose big pieces of bedrock, pushing them and piling them up in big moraines. Harder rock as found in the archipelago of Solund was not eroded so much.

After some time the glaciers also eroded their way towards the ocean. The climax in this process must have been the moment when the water under the glacier gushed up and was replaced by ocean water. In this way the first fjord was formed and opened. At Rutletangane in the western part of the Sognefjord, the ice sheet was not so thick, and for this reason there was less

⮞ *View of the Aurlandsfjord.*

erosion by the glacier, thus forming a threshold. It is these shallow thresholds and deep troughs that are characteristic lengthwise features and criteria of valleys and fjords mainly formed by glacial erosion.

The contact with the warm ocean water of the Gulf Stream makes the Sognefjord a unique heat reservoir. The main fjord never freezes to ice. Ice is a problem only in a few fjord branches. The oceanic breath reaches far inland. To the west, on the same latitude as Sogn, lies the southern tip of Greenland and the sub-arctic areas in northern Canada and Alaska. To the east, Siberia is on the same latitude as well. In January the mean temperature in Sogn is 20–22 degrees centigrade higher than in corresponding areas in Siberia, Canada, and Alaska.

The Sognefjord is one of the longest fjords in the world. From Solund to Skjolden it covers a distance of some 200 kilometres. The width varies, but it is five kilometres at its widest. The fjord is relatively shallow at the mouth of the fjord – about 160 metres. At the entrance to the Vadheimsfjord it reaches its maximum depth of 1306 metres. The difference in altitude between the lowest point in the fjord and the highest mountain peak is about 3000 metres in some places along the Sognefjord.

PEOPLE ON THE MOVE

From Sognesjøen we get a glimpse of the ocean to the west – the North Sea. On the island of Utvær in Solund, there are some marks in the bedrock that are geological phenomena. But, according to popular belief, these marks are traces left by Vikings when they sharpened their swords before heading west across the ocean on their raids. The Viking Age lasted about 250 years, from 800 to 1066 when king Harald Hardråde (Hardruler) fell at the battle of Stamford Bridge in England. It was precisely at Utvær that Harald organized and prepared his forces before setting out on his raid across the North Sea to England. From this island the crossing to Shetland took only a few days. Then he turned south by way of the Orkneys and across a short stretch of open sea before anchoring up off the Hebrides. In women's graves from the Viking Age a number of objects of Irish origin have been found, proof of an early connection between the villages of Sogn and Ireland.

The Viking raids were in fact part of the migration that started in the 7th century. The petty kings and chieftains sought land on Iceland. The cultural and intellectual elite emigrated. The Icelanders emerged as a people with a culture rarely seen in Europe in the 11th century. The island was a free state, without king, having a unique political form of government. Their culture, based on the written language and recorded on vellum, reached high and

⇨ *This is how the artist Hans Dahl imagined Leiv Eiriksson step ashore in America.*

far. The books by Snorri Sturluson may be considered as part of the world literature. His statue at Dreggen in Bergen is marvellous.

In the 19th century a new type of migration started from the villages in Sogn. This had clear parallels to the migrations that took place in the Viking Age. This time, though, the people from Sogn headed for the United States. The first person to emigrate was Per Ivarson Undi from Vik. He may have got knowledge of America through relatives from Voss. He left in 1839, and his departure had a dramatic effect. In the course of a period of 20 years between 1846 and 1865, a quarter of the population of central and inner Sogn emigrated to America. In contrast, from the outer area of Sogn, fewer than 100 people left in the same period.

There is some disagreement among historians as to the main cause of this emigration, but there are indications that the situation was similar to that of the migration in the 8th and 9th centuries. The fjord with its narrow band of arable land between the sea and the steep mountainsides could no longer provide enough food for the population boom during those years. In 1769, some 19,000 people lived in Sogn. In 1865, the number of inhabitants had almost doubled to 36,000. This is actually 10,000 more than the present population of Sogn. One reason for this substantial population increase in the first half of the 19th century was the fact that the potato had now become a staple food. The potato gave a good, reliable crop every year. Parallel to the use of the potato as a food crop, the coastal areas experienced incredible catches of herring from the early 19th century. Our villages were "flooded" with calories, vitamins and proteins. Infant mortality was reduced. People's life expectancy became longer. The population increase also resulted in the emergence of an underclass of numerous people, the crofters, which may explain the strong support for the organised labour movement, especially in the eastern areas of Sogn.

Were these emigrants from Sogn better off in the USA? This question has been raised by the historian Rasmus Sunde in his doctoral thesis. The basis for his research is the significant emigration from Vik in the period between 1839 and 1864. During this period more than 3300 persons emigrated. In 1835, the population of Vik had reached 3140. Sunde's research findings are remarkable. He showed that the American side had a significantly lower life expectancy at birth compared to those who chose not to emigrate. The emigrated people from Vik also married earlier and got many children. Marrying early was probably the reason why births out of wedlock hardly occurred in America, while this was a quite common occurrence in Vik as well as elsewhere in Sogn.

< *The dockside represents the intersection between the local community and the outside world.*

THE MAGICAL LIFE ALONG THE FJORD

Living close to the fjord makes for a special lifestyle. The people who live there have a high life expectancy, in fact amongst the highest in the world. This phenomenon has never been properly studied. As we do not have sufficient knowledge why local people live such long lives, there seems to be something magical about it. Could it simply be the clean water in the rivers,

Nobody seems to know why people along the Sognefjord enjoy such a high life expectancy. Could the fjord be the life-giving force?

the fresh air, the old gamalost, the tasty fish in the fjord, the delicious mutton and the sweet blueberries on the hillsides that contribute to the good health of people? Or, could the genes there be different from those found elsewhere in the country or in Europe for that matter? Could there be any connection to the ability of the people to adapt to the natural rhythm of life? We have no answer.

When the first settlers cleared the beaches, they often used the rocks and stones to build a wall out into the sea. This made it possible for people to step ashore from the boat without getting their feet wet. Today, deer and wild goats feed on the seaweed washed up on the foreshore. From these stonewalls and out to a depth of about 10–12 metres we find an extremely rich marine life. This zone is of vital importance as a feeding ground for small fish. Small crustaceans such as amphipods, shrimp, and barnacles grow in abundance. Similarly, we find green crabs, snails and seashells of various species and sizes. Larger fish prey on the crustaceans and the small fry. There is food for everyone in the fjord. There cannot be any better larder.

Sitting on a dock can be an exploration into the diversity of our marine life. Maybe you will discover the eyes of a common dab peeping up from the sand bottom. A shrimp changes its spots and stripes to match perfectly the background. The colours and the patterns of many fish species can change to make them indistinguishable from their environment.

Then we may suddenly hear heavy breathing from the fjord. A porpoise breaks the calm surface of the fjord. It comes up for air. Porpoises belong to an older family compared to the ocean-going dolphins, but porpoises have a blunt rounded snout in contrast to the characteristic slender beaklike snout of the dolphins. The porpoises are dark grey but lighter on the sides and with a white underside. They may reach a length of 1.9 metres and can weigh up to 65 kilos. They chase shoals of small fish, individually if there is little food, but co-operating in groups when the small fish are plentiful.

In the fjord we may also come across the seal – a shy and easily frightened hunter. It helps itself greedily to the fish in the fjord. It is an extremely shrewd hunter. Its fishing technique infuriates the fishermen because it patrols the mackerel nets and eats the fish as soon as it is caught in the net, leaving only the heads of the fish. The otter is also an accomplished hunter, and the population of seal and otter has increased significantly in recent years.

As smolt the salmon swims out into the fjord before migrating further east to feed into the ocean. When it is ready to spawn, it returns to its native river.

⊳*A killer whale in a playful mood in the fjord.*

THE SMALL TOWN OF HØYANGER
– IDYLL AND INDUSTRY

At the head of the Høyangsfjord lies Høyanger, the industrial town which may symbolise the transformation of Norwegian society in the early 20th century. In 1913, Høyanger had a population of 120, living on 13 small farms and four crofter's farms. However, when A/S Norsk Aluminium Company (NACO) between 1916 and 1920 constructed a hydroelectric power station and an aluminium plant at this isolated place, a new era was introduced. The place experienced a population boom, and in 1920, Høyanger had 953 inhabitants. A decade later, this had increased to 2216, and it has remained at this level ever since.

The landscape itself explains the industrial success story in Høyanger. Water falling down these steep mountainsides has enormous power and this has been used to produce electricity since the early 20th century. The Sogn region is one of the country's major producers of hydroelectric energy, supplying cities and built-up areas all over southern Norway.

Arriving in Høyanger on a summer's day is really like visiting a different world. We expect a Norwegian industrial town. However, what we see is an idyllic small town by the fjord with parks and villa streets lined with linden trees. We see a fantastic profusion of flowers, recently bought art in the public spaces, a modern worker's monument centrally located in front of the Community Centre where Water cascades over white stone. The City Gate, where the Industrial Town Museum is located, shows us the architectural idea behind the small town. From the City Gate we have a direct view of the church that was designed by the architect Arnstein Arneberg. By the way, the church was the last public building that the workers of Høyanger built, completed as late as in 1960. "Folkets Hus" (literally: the people's house), the socialist meeting-place, was built as early as in 1918. This fact reveals a lot about one of the strangest phenomena in our regional history: When Høyanger was established as an industrial town, nearly all the workers came from the neighbouring villages. Practically overnight, they became socialists and communists all of them.

Maybe if we make a stop in Storgata, the main street, we can see the statue of "Mother and Child". Further down the street sits "The Passenger", an old woman waiting for a bus or boat. Artistic decoration is a characteristic feature of Høyanger, the shining small town without official city status. Høyanger is an unusual place, still situated like a modern and transformed industrial island in an ocean of small farms. Today many of these small farms on

> *The Høyanger church was completed in 1960 and was designed by the renowned architect Arnstein Arneberg.*

the northern shore of the Sognefjord are kept in active use precisely because the local industry can provide supplementary workplaces.

ISOLATED HAMLETS

The living conditions along the Sognefjord may differ from one place to another. Out by the coast fish farming is an important source of income. Further inland – along the many fjord branches with their high and wild mountains – we encounter astonishing fertile land with its profusion of spring blossoms and its autumnal fruit harvest. High up on the mountainsides we can discern the incredible mountain farms with their commanding views, whose names still reflect imaginary mythical creatures such as trolls and wood nymphs. There are still people living in isolated hamlets along the fjord. A case in point is Måren at the entrance to the Høyangsfjord. The sensitive and strange poet Ivar Ovredal lives there, and, according to him, one of the most exotic experiences Europe has to offer nowadays is to live in isolated places. Here you can find peace of mind, and your thoughts are free and unstrained. Today the boat "Solrenning" connects the villages on either side of the fjord.

The Finnafjord, which means 'the deserted fjord', is also wild and isolated. It cuts in from the main fjord to the south. A boat excursion to Finnabotn is one of the most popular and exotic tourist attractions in Sogn. The farm, Finden, is located by the narrow current leading into the calm water of Finnabotn, surrounded by almost vertical mountainsides. Laila Lilleøren and Lars Finden live on this farm. In a matter of a few years, they have developed a tourist concept that is now highly praised. A key element in this development was the designation of the mountain area called Stølsheimen as a landscape preservation area. Whereas most people in the country think that protection of natural areas and exploitable resources constitutes a threat to rural industries, this couple has asked for protection and created their own workplaces, where precisely the protection status and local exploitation of resources make up the framework of their business activities.

Whereas Synnøve Finden, who came from this hamlet, became a household name in Norway for her cheese, Laila and Lars have made a name for themselves because of their venison patties. The deer is hunted on the precipitous mountainsides near Finden. The meat gets its wild taste from the hills of western Norway, and it melts on the tongue. – No witchcraft recipe is needed to make venison patties, says Laila. – All you have to do is to make them of freshly ground meat and keep them at arm's length from any so-called venison spices. It is a mortal sin to make large quantities and then

< *Høyanger is an unusually well-regulated local community between fjord and mountains.*

Finnafjorden is an isolated place. A voyage to Finnabotn is an exotic experience.

freeze them. That will not work. Besides, you need a quiet setting and much time to make good food. This also applies to venison patties which are a regular main course in the 2000 dinners served here every year, she adds.

FIVE IN STAVE AND FIVE IN STONE

In Sogn there are five stave churches and five stone churches. Borgund is certainly our best-known stave church, but the oldest one is located at Urnes.

The Urnes church was placed on the UNESCO World Heritage List in 1980. The present church probably dates back to 1130, but some building materials are taken from an even older building with ornamental carving consisting of intertwined loops and slender animal forms. These carvings constitute a special ornamentation group in our art history, now known as the Urnes style. Some people even claim that certain elements in the Urnes church may stem from a heathen place of worship and a runic inscription on a wooden rivet from the 9th century has also been found on the site. There can be no doubt that the church is situated on an ancient cult site, and heathen motifs, snakes and other types of animal ornamentation are found in the church portals.

In 1851, a law was passed to the effect that the churches should be big enough to house three tenths of the congregation. Thus, what with the increased population, it became necessary to construct new and bigger churches to replace the old ones. And, according to the prevailing ideology of the new times, more light was required in the new churches than had been the case in the old ones. The Age of Enlightenment demanded light everywhere, also in churches.

Both the Hove stone church and the Hopperstad stave church in Vik were dangerously close to demolition in the 1850s and later. The eminent politician and resourceful vicar Harald Ulrik Sverdrup in Balestrand was partly responsible for tearing down three old stave churches in his parish in the 1850s. The old churches at Tjugum, Vangsnes and Fjærland were sacrificed for the new light. In Vik, on the other hand, things turned out differently. The "church saviour" Peter Andreas Blix (1831–1901) entered the stage. He restored the two churches of Hopperstad and Hove. From 1885 onwards, Blix came to Vik every summer to take charge of the restoration work. In 1888, the Hove stone church was completed, followed three years later by the Hopperstad

The Hove stone church was built about 1170.

⊱ *The Hopperstad stave church dates back to the first half of the 12ʰ century. The architect Peter Andreas Blix used the Borgund stave church as a model when he restored Hopperstad in the late 19ʰ century.*

Reconstructed woman's costume from the early 19ᵗʰ century. The baby wears a baptismal dress from the early 20ᵗʰ century with a reconstructed baptismal cap from the 19ᵗʰ century.

⋞ The animal ornament in the northern portal of the Urnes stave church is also found on the Norwegian 50 øre coin.

stave church which was modelled after the Borgund stave church. Through his work Blix set the standard for the restoration work of other churches.

In addition to Hopperstad, Borgund, and Urnes, we find stave churches in Gaupne and Kaupanger. Medieval stone churches are found in Aurland, Leikanger, at Hove in Vik, and on Kvamsøy, the only island in the Sognefjord. In Luster we find the beautiful, richly decorated Dale church.

THE MAGICAL CHEESE

One of the explanations for the high life expectancy in Sogn is said to be the gamalost (literally: old cheese). The Vik dairy is today, the country's sole producer of this cheese. The dairy has a staff of 18, producing more than 150 tonnes of cheese annually. Gamalost is probably our oldest variety of cheese. The oldest recorded description was made by bishop Johan Gunnerus in 1774. Hanna Winsnes refers to this cheese in her book of recipes from 1848. There is also reason to believe that the Vikings included gamalost as part of their provisions for their voyages. The cheese may have got its name from the times when it was produced on the mountain farms. At that time they could not apply any mould culture, and it took several weeks until the cheese was ripened. Nowadays the whole process takes only two weeks until the strongly flavoured cheese is ready for sale. In eastern Norway this cheese was called "Bergen gamalost", which tells us that the cheese was associated with western Norway, transported on jekts to Bergen and resold again.

Gamalost has a reputation of being a remedy against the common cold and coughing. Some people are convinced that it also strengthens the sexual power of men. At any rate, people from Sogn show virility. Contemporary sources from the 19ᵗʰ century are quite clear on this point: it could be a problem for the local people to keep their erotic desires under control. Those who came from the outside world to observe the rural communities called the people along the fjord immoral and promiscuous. For this reason, it might be a good idea to market gamalost as a love cheese par excellence. The cheese contains only about 1% fat, and is without salt or sugar. It caused a sensation when it was discovered that the cheese also contained chitosan. This is a substance derived from chitin which can reduce the level of choles-

"Gamalost" (Old cheese) is a unique speciality from western Norway.

terol in the blood. In order to promote the sale of this cheese, the Norwegian Gamalost Association was founded in 1986. Since 1996, an annual festival honouring this unique cheese has been held in Vik.

Before industrial dairy production of gamalost was started, the cheese was made of self-soured skimmed milk, and natural bacteria took care of the ripening process. Today the milk is stored in 30,000-litre tanks outside the dairy. Then the milk is pumped into tanks in the cheese factory, heated to a temperature of about 21 degrees centigrade, and a certain amount of lactic acid bacteria added to make it sour. Machines separate the curd from the whey. The curd is then transferred into moulds, which are lowered into tanks of boiling whey and left there for two to three hours. Afterwards a mould culture (a fungus called mucor mucedo) is applied. Latin is the language of medicine, and gamalost is medicine. The fungus grows from the outside into the core of the cheese, thereby ripening it. After about two weeks the cheese is packed and is ready for sale. Visiting Sogn without tasting gamalost is in fact a wasted journey.

HOTELS AND SMALL TOWNS

The great revolution in terms of communication came with the establishment in 1858, of "Fylkesbaatane" – the county's own shipping company – with its headquarters in Bergen. "Fylkesbaatane" represented something revolutionary in our country. The county community owned and operated the ships, not private persons or companies. The steamship traffic opened up the county. The boats called regularly at various stops. Foreign tourists came first to Bergen, especially from England, and travelled on to the villages and small towns on the Sognefjord. Providing accommodation and services for tourists became a new important source of income for many people. The fjord, the mountains and the glacier, became the new fashionable destinations for the people of industrialized Europe.

The great leap or major upswing in tourism took place in the 1890s, and

> *The English church in Balestrand belongs to the Church of England and is under the spiritual jurisdiction of the Bishop of Gibraltar. It was built in 1897 and was designed in a stave church style by the architect Jens Zetlitz Kielland.*

A rare encounter between nature and culture as the killer whales glide past the centre of Balestrand.

the future looked exceedingly bright. New hotels sprang up with fancy towers and turrets, dormers, and verandas. Many of these huge hotels are today considered architectural gems. The main building of Kvikne's Hotel in Balestrand was completed in 1913, and this is today among the biggest wooden buildings in northern Europe.

In connection with the docks and the hotels new rural communities developed. The dockside became the main meeting-place between the village and the outside world. Suitcases, barrels of herring, sacks of flour, salt and

syrup constituted a delightful mixture, creating a very special atmosphere. The dock had an important social function, also for the layabout.

Close to the dock new businesses developed such as the post office, telegraph station, grocer's shop, dairy and bakery. Tourism generated much money for the rural communities. It was possible to make money by taking tourists out in white-painted rowboats on the fjord, or by selling strawberries and raspberries. Salmon was much in demand by the hotel kitchens as salmon and strawberries were the main items on the set menu. This actually

⚘ *The world famous Swiss-style façade of Kvikne's Hotel. The hotel dates back to 1877.*

⚘ *In the Høivik hall in the hotel we find the chair that the German Kaiser Wilhelm II was sitting in when the First World War broke out.*

led to many complaints by the tourists. Moving from one hotel to another in western Norway, their dinner consisted in most cases of the inevitable salmon and strawberries. This optimism in the tourist trade lasted up to the outbreak of the First World War. Germans came in ever-increasing numbers, tempted by the newspaper articles of Kaiser Wilhelm II's annual fjord excursions to Norway.

Kaiser Wilhelm II, Imperator Rex (IR), Emperor of Germany and King of

Prussia, gave Sogn its reputation as a tourist destination and created the romantic "Emperor Era". The Fridtjof statue at Vangsnes and the king Bele statue in Balestrand are both gifts from this strange man who ended his life in the Netherlands in 1941. There are still place names associated with the Kaiser's quiet walks along the shores and in outlying areas. His yacht "The Hohenzollern" plied the fjords of western Norway every summer, from his first visit to Lærdal on 10 July, 1889, until his last visit on 30 July, 1914. Then Europe was on the brink of war. The Kaiser was fond of travelling, and the abbreviation of his official title – IR – was jokingly interpreted as "immer reisefertig" – always ready to travel.

There is an air of aristocracy associated with the Kaiser's visits to Sogn. The Kaiser was a warm admirer of professor Hans Dahl and his art. In all, he bought 63 paintings by the artist, and he was very much influenced by what we may term the German artistic fantasies in the 19th century. These fantasies were given free rein in the speech the Kaiser gave at Vangsnes on 31 July, 1913, at the unveiling ceremony of the Fridtjof statue. The Kaiser spoke of a common-Germanic tribe and the strong blood ties between Scandinavia and Germany. His speech was definitely marked by the spirit of the age.

In Sogn there are many cultural monuments created by tourism. St. Olaf Church, the English church in Balestrand, is a case in point. The English vicar's daughter, Margaret Green, was a mountaineering pioneer in Norway. She came to Balestrand in the late 1880s, where she became acquainted with the hotel man and mountain guide Knut Kvikne. They married in the Tjugum church, but Margaret died from tuberculosis a couple of years later. Her last will was that an Anglican church should be built in Balestrand. This church was completed in 1897, and ever since, the church has been a treasured place of worship for travellers to Balholm and Sogn. Every year about

> *Villa Strandheim was Hans Dahl's summer residence, and the Berlin city coat of arms has a prominent place on the house. In the winter months Hans Dahl lived in Berlin.*

~
ARTISTIC GEMS AT
THE SOGNEFJORD AQUARIUM

Woodcarving, local-historical motifs, and watercolour painting were used by Magnus Sande to express his artistic vision. His works are found in Galleri Munken in Balestrand. The displayed works of art depict life on the docks,

going to church in Undredal, as well as scenes of salmon catching. Everything is made with an exquisite technique, and the material he uses for carving is lime-wood. Magnus Sande is originally a hotel man by trade, and he owned and ran Kringsjå Hotel until 1975 when his son took over.

10 000 persons write their names in the guestbook, and many tourists seek this place for quiet contemplation and prayers throughout the summer.

Today the Norwegian fjord hotels are a mixture of wood and concrete. Concrete was introduced in the 1960s after the old Stalheim hotel had burned down and some 20 American tourists lost their lives. Through state investment schemes, a comprehensive renovation of the Norwegian hotels was carried out. Fire prevention was one of the key elements. But the work had to be completed within a strict economic framework. At that time Norway was not a rich country. Consequently, the resources had to be targeted to build functional hotels, power stations, power lines and reservoirs, schools and universities.

Bearing this in mind, we can understand more easily, why these fireproof, functional, and inexpensive concrete buildings – mostly used for bedrooms – were constructed at so many of our tourist resorts during that period. Later it has turned out that the construction of all these new concrete buildings was a very sound investment for the tourist industry. The hotels could cater for a drastically increased number of guests, the concrete buildings required little maintenance, as well as having moderate operational costs. The generated income from these concrete hotel buildings can be used to maintain, develop and renew the old wooden buildings.

THE FJÆRLANDSFJORD

At Balestrand we can take a side trip to Fjærland. In the tourist season, we can make a day return voyage on a ferry. The Fjærlandsfjord opens up at the

> ✣ *Fjærland is probably one of the most idyllic places for book-lovers in Norway. The Norwegian Book Town was established in 1995.*

Fjærland

Like most glaciers the Bøyabreen glacier in Fjærland has receded and melted much in the last few years.

≼ *The fairy-tale exterior of Hotel Mundal in Fjærland. The hotel was built in 1891 and was designed by the architect Peter Andreas Blix.*

point of Veganeset, a low, spruce-forested peninsula. Veganeset was formerly a place of execution for the villages of Sogn. Thieves, murderers, witches and other riff-raff were beheaded, and their heads were displayed on stakes. The old communication artery between the regions of Sogn and Sunnfjord passed the point of Veganeset. This route came across the pass at Sværaskardet, down to Farnes, and then continued by boat to Hella.

The Fjærlandsfjord stretches 27 kilometres inland. The Fjærlandsfjord ends within sight of the Jostedal glacier, the largest glacier on the European mainland. This glacier covers an area of nearly 500 sq km, in places reaching a thickness of 500 metres. Fjærland is an ideal place for studying at close range how the glacier and the rivers interact to build new land. The delta extends further out every year, and the vegetation follows suit. The wetland areas in the inner fjord basins where the glacial rivers enter the sea are among our most productive biotopes. At the Bøyaøyri delta, close to 90 different bird species have been registered.

Fjærland did not get any road connection to the outside world until 1986, and before that year, the sea was the only communication artery. In this way the village under the Jostedal glacier turned into a very special community with a close-knit social and economic structure. The village had its own bank and dairy, school, hotel, and shops. Today the activities in the village of Fjærland are dominated by two very special institutions: the Norwegian Booktown and the Norwegian Glacier Museum. Both these initiatives are good exam-

73

Fruit blossom at Hermansverk, Leikanger.

ples of the creative attitudes always present among the people of Fjærland.

The proximity to the glacier has attracted tourists to Fjærland ever since the latter part of the 19th century. Brita Mundal, her husband Olaus Dahle and her brother Mikkel had been running a pension in the village. Mikkel was a guide on the glacier. They commissioned the architect Peter Andreas Blix to design a hotel. The resulting Hotel Mundal was built in a neo-Gothic style with steep roofs and very pointed gable walls. The hotel was opened on 29 June, 1891, and the most characteristic architectural feature is the imposing corner tower with a cone-shaped roof and semi-circular verandas around both floors. Even if some changes have been made, the hotel has kept its fairy-tale charm.

Brita Mundal and another woman from the village, Klaudine Skarestad,

both made handicraft products of excellent artistic quality. They were both weavers, working according to traditional handicraft methods. This became a welcome supplementary source of income for women in Sogn. Tourists were their primary customers, but the women also travelled to Oslo to sell their products. Throughout the long winter months the women knitted sweaters and mittens, and wove runners for sale in the summer months.

LEIKANGER

The orchards of Leikanger enjoy such a favourable climate that apricots and peaches can be grown outside greenhouses. The Plant Research Station at

THE BERRY SUCCESS

On a July evening in the early 20th century, two barrels of raspberries were left unsold on the dock at Sørheim on the Lusterfjord. People from the village had picked the berries and expected to be paid for their efforts. The young couple Kari and Nils Lerum had been running their shop for only a few years, and they did not want to disappoint their neighbours. But what were they to do with the berries? Well, they found a way out. Kari made raspberry jam, preserved it and later sold it. Kari knew a thing or two about making jam. Indeed, it is her recipe, which is now being used close to a century later, forming the basis for the commercial success under the trademark of "Bestemor (Grandmother) Lerum". In many other later instances, the Lerum family has always demonstrated their God-given talent of turning a problem into a success.

At Sørheim the fjord was covered with ice in wintertime, thus making it hard to get their products out of the village. As a result, in 1919, Kari and Nils Lerum then moved their production activity to Sogndal where it still is today. There has been a certain feeling of optimism within the berry industry in recent years. Orchards are cleared of fruit trees and raspberries are planted instead.

Much of the innovation within berry growing production has taken place at the Njøs Plant Research Station in Leikanger. Research and development has led to hardy berry varieties with improved crops and larger berries. Leikanger is an ideal place for this kind of development work. The village is situated like an open hand facing south.

Njøs hybridizes and experiments with these Mediterranean fruits in an attempt to cultivate them so far north.

The fjord is a remarkable heat basin. The problem with the outdoor cultivation of apricots and peaches at Leikanger, is the fact that the blossoming occurs so early on these trees that there are not enough insects to pollinate properly.

– This means that we get good crops only every five years on average. A commercial cultivation of these Mediterranean fruits is so far not viable, says the plant researcher Stein Harald Hjeltnes. – However, we are still doing research to produce hardier varieties, but the early blossoming still remains our main problem.

The Njøs station does not experiment only with apricots and peaches. This research farm has had an enormous influence on horticulture and fruit-growing in Sogn, and many varieties of berries and fruit have been given local names.

Fridtjof and Ingeborg are the main characters in the well-known Fridtjof's

Saga, and for this reason the Plant Research Station chose these two names for our new pear varieties.

Leikanger is the actual county capital of Sogn og Fjordane as both the regional state bodies and the county administration have their main offices there.

FIMREITE

Fimreite is situated at the entrance to the Norafjord. This place has written its name into our history books. Around midday on 15 June 1184, the battle commenced that many historians consider being the most important and decisive in our national history. This battle was the final confrontation between king Sverre, the man from the distant Faroe Isles, and Magnus Erlingson who represented the nobility, the upper class and the church. Before nightfall 2,000 men had lost their lives.

What the battle at Fimreite reveals, is above all the supreme leadership qualities of king Sverre as a military strategist. All the odds were against him. As long as Magnus Erlingson lived, Sverre could not count on any support in the west of Norway. His local sheriffs in Sogn had demanded a feast for the yule-tide holiday – food and beer – and they wanted to "drink the yule-tide" at Kaupanger and Sogndal. But the Sogn people refused to provide them with any food and drink. Sverre was furious. In the following early spring he sailed south from Trondheim with big, new ships and headed into the Sognefjord. The villagers of Sogndal were heavily fined, but they refused to pay and fled up in the mountains.

Sverre's response was to let his men raid the village and the small market town of Kaupanger. When there was nothing left of any value to be taken in

Aerial view of Fimreite.

Fimreite has a familiar historical ring to its name for all Norwegians. The battle that took place there in 1184 was a turning-point in Norwegian history.

Sogndal and Kaupanger, Sverre ordered his men to set fire to all the houses. The churches at Stedje (Sogndal) and Kaupanger, however, were spared as they were covered with wet ships' sails before the houses around were set on fire. At Fimreite – on his way out of the fjord from Sogndal – Sverre was caught off guard for the first time during these war activities. Some of his ships were still anchored up at Kaupanger, and Magnus came sailing into

the fjord with a fleet of no less than 26 ships. He had got reinforcements from Denmark and the area around the Oslofjord. In addition, the people of western Norway were on his side. Escape was out of the question. Sverre was trapped in the hostile territory of Sogn with only 14 ships.

Before the battle, Sverre held one of his famous speeches where he urged his men to fight. He promised his men that whoever killed a nobleman,

would himself become one. He concluded his speech with the words: "Today you shall send a king to Hell!" Sverre let his ships sail individually without tying them together as was the custom. In this way it was easier to attack the weak points in Magnus's fleet. For his part, Sverre boarded a small rowboat in order to organize and position his ships better. He tried in vain to get back on his own ship again but the hail of arrows was so dense that he was forced to go ashore instead. Would he run away if the battle were lost?

From land he could observe how his strategy worked. One by one Magnus's smaller ships were boarded by Sverre's men, and the crews crowded together on the bigger ships. And suddenly Magnus's men were panic-stricken and scrambled from the remaining smaller ships over to the bigger ships. Three of these ships sank. The weight of the extra men coupled with the lack of space onboard made fighting impossible. King Magnus and his men jumped overboard and drowned. They were picked up from the sea and taken to Bergen where they were buried at the church called Kristkyrkja.

SOGNDALSFJØRA – THE CENTRE OF SOGNDAL

As with so many places in Sogn, the town of Sogndal should be approached from the fjord. We can see the small houses and the narrow streets leading up to square at Fossatunet. This was the place where the so-called sea crofters lived, those who did not own any property. They were numerous in Sogndal, at Lærdalsøyri and Vikøyri. Growing up in this environment was the notorious Gjest Bårdsen Sogndalsfjæren (1791–1849). He was a master thief and a prison-breaker. No fewer than 57 times did he escape from prison. He was

☻ *Sogndal is today an educational centre with about 2,000 students.*

Sogndalsfjøra with the Hofslund Hotel in the foreground.

helped by locals everywhere. In the public imagination he became Norway's counterpart to Robin Hood, the man who stole from the rich and gave to the poor. In addition, he earned a reputation as an unrivalled lady's man.

In 1827 he was incarcerated for life at Akershus in Oslo where he wrote his autobiography. Gjest Bårdsen has indeed been a controversial person to put it mildly. Some of the myths have fallen, but a wonderful film about him and his life has been produced. Both the film production and the performance

of the actors are an outstanding achievement in Norwegian film history. The house where Gjest lived in Sogndal has now been rebuilt and restored in the old sea-crofters' environment after endless debates and various views on this strange man. Today Sogndal is a regional commercial and educational centre. It is also famous for its football team that has played some years in the top division and even played in a cup final.

The collection of farm implements and tools at Sogn Folkemuseum is one of the most important in the country. Some 30,000 objects and artefacts as well as 40 buildings have been preserved.

KAUPANGER

From Kaupanger it is possible to catch a ferry to Lærdal and Gudvangen in the summer season. Around the natural harbour of the Amlabukta bay, the oldest market town in Sogn – the so-called "Lusa-kaupang" – was situated. There we find the Kaupanger manor which is the largest property in private hands in the county. For many years this manor was a nobleman's residence. For close to three centuries the property has been owned by the Knagenhjelm family. At Kaupanger we find the biggest of the five stave churches in Sogn, probably completed in the late 12th century. As a result of a rather rough restoration effort in 1862, the church lost much of its original character, but this has partly been rectified in the 1965 restoration.

The Heiberg Collections – Sogn Folkemuseum is situated at Kaupangerskogen, but the Sogn Fjord Museum is located down by the bay. Kaupangerskogen is now one of the most expansive industrial estates in the county with Lerum's gigantic industrial complex and the establishment of many car dealer facilities. Next door to the Heiberg Collections we find the large tourist facility of Vesterland.

LÆRDALSØYRI – SO FAR DOES THE BREATH FROM BERGEN REACH

There are few places where the breath of influence from Bergen is more visible than in Lærdal. The old centre of Lærdal – Lærdalsøyri – was Bergen's extended arm, as it were, to the eastern valleys of Hallingdal and Valdres. Around 1840, there were even plans to build a city there. This city idea was founded on the east-west trade. The Lærdal Market was a meeting-place for people from the eastern valleys, the fjords, the coast, and from Bergen, where goods were bartered without using money. It must also be added that this market also served as an important cultural intersection for the dissemination and exchange of folklore and folk music.

Many people made a good living on this transit trade at Lærdalsøyri. One of these was Jan Henrik Nitter Hansen, whose family roots were in Luster. His parents were Tøger Anderson Nitter and Mari Henriksdotter Nitter. Jan

Henrik was a rich and enterprising man. He envisaged a new Lærdal city with streets, houses, shops and workshops from the harbour all the way up to the place where the present county hospital is located. In the 1840s, he built a residence called Hansegarden on the outskirts of Lærdalsøyri. The design and architectural details of this house have obvious links to Bergen. Most likely, Jan Hansen had dreams of turning Lærdal into a sort of Bergen in miniature. The architect Johan Lindstrøm has demonstrated the many similar features between Hansegarden and the summerhouse called Frydenlund now displayed at the museum of Gamle Bergen (Old Bergen). This is probably the best collection of wooden houses in the whole country. At Gamle Bergen people can feel at home and reminisce, also people from the rural areas.

Strolling along the street of Øyragata at Lærdalsøyri is a fantastic experience. Here we encounter the first effects of liberalism in Norway. Prior to 1850, it was necessary to be a citizen of Bergen in order to do business in Sogn. The gradual weakening of the monopoly status of the cities, led to a positive development and growth for the small towns. Lærdalsøyri is an excellent case in point. But Lærdalsøyri never got any city status because the Lærdal Market lost most of its economic position when Bergen took complete economic control of Sogn by the establishment of Fylkesbaatane – the county's own steamship company. Finally, the Lærdal Market was reduced in importance to a place where horses were bought and sold, and where people from various neighbouring districts could meet to show off their fighting talents with knives. Fighting with knives has never led to any building of new cities.

THE SALMON FJORD

Wild salmon are hatched in the salmon rivers in our inner fjord branches. The river running through the valley of Lærdal is the best known of these and has been called the "queen" among our rivers. As smolt the salmon swims out into the fjord, passing bays, points and currents before it migrates further east to feed in the ocean. When it is ready to spawn, the time has come to return to its native river.

The innermost part of the Sognefjord is today categorized under the term "national salmon fjords". The stocks of wild salmon have been catastrophically reduced in the past few decades. Comprehensive restrictions have been

The old centre of Lærdalsøyri shows building environments from the 18th and the 19th centuries.

⊳ *The river of Lærdalselvi erodes its own course from the mountains to the fjord.*

implemented on all types of fishing, and the Norwegian authorities use police forces to prevent illegal salmon fishing with nets. This initiative, however, has not proved to be enough.

A government report from 1999 concluded that it was necessary to introduce the concept of "national salmon fjords" in order to save what little was left of the wild salmon stocks. According to the researchers, when smolt is on its way to the ocean, it mingles with lice-covered escaped salmon from the pens of the fish farms. This louse (Lepeophtheirus salmonis) will eventually kill the wild salmon. In addition, the escaped farmed salmon have gone up the rivers and mixed with wild salmon. The national salmon fjords, then, must be completely free of salmon-farming facilities, which has led to heated conflicts between the fish-farming industry and the wild salmon enthusiasts. Now the Sognefjord has become a national salmon fjord.

In the last decade the wild salmon has become such an endangered genetic species that it was felt to be necessary to document what wild salmon was, and what it had meant to the local economy of the Sogn villages. Consequently, the Norwegian Wild Salmon Centre was established at Lærdalsøyri close to the old cluster of small houses.

THE WORLD HERITAGE SITE OF THE NÆRØYFJORD

The Aurlandsfjord has everything that a Norwegian fjord ought to have. The altitude difference between the bottom of the Aurlandsfjord and the mountaintop of Bleia is about 2700 metres. The vertical crag of Beitelen marks the "crossfjords" of the Aurlandsfjord and the Nærøyfjord. Just to the north of Beitelen we find the boat stop called "Mid-fjord". It has been said that the places in Norway that are best known in Japan are Flåm and "Mid-fjord". At this latter point boats and ferries meet and connect out on the open fjord. If you arrive by express boat from Bergen going to Flåm, you can change boats simply by stepping onboard the ferry for Gudvangen. Formerly, up to five boats could meet and connect there. Worried passengers could only watch in horror as their suitcases were thrown from one boat to another. It has even happened that husband and wife have ended up at the two different destinations of Gudvangen and Flåm.

Archeological finds from the neolithic (later part of the) Stone Age indicate that there was a highly developed culture based on hunting and fishing in the mountains and the areas around the Nærøyfjord. From the Iron Age and the Middle Ages a number of big pitfalls, guiding fences, as well as a series of cairns and built-up positions for using bows and arrows have been registered. The reindeer in the mountains played an important part in the constant struggle to find enough food. Along the Nærøyfjord we also find the burial mounds at Holmo.

The Ramsøy farm. The Nærøyfjord was designated a World Heritage Site also because of its well-preserved cultural landscape.

Previously the fjord was an important part of the communication system in the region. Today tourists are the main users of the ferry connections between Kaupanger, Flåm, and Gudvangen.

We find many traces of human settlement and activities in more recent years as well. The interplay between a wild and untamed countryside and a cultural landscape with a minimum of encroachments is unique. The variations are infinite. There are birch copses, hayfields, pastures, and areas for harvesting foliage as a supplementary fodder for animals. Pollarded trees – where branches have been cut off to encourage new growth – are still standing as a reminder of the former method of harvesting and drying leaves for fodder. Traces of the old settlements reveal agricultural methods in harmony with nature all the way from the fjord up to the mountains. There are mountain (summer) farms, outlying hay barns, stone walls, piles of stones from clearing the fields, and tracks criss-crossing the mountainsides. The traditional building environment is the old cluster

of farmhouses, with later additions of more modern houses. Today the cultural landscape resembles a colourful quilt of orchards, gardens, and fields.

Along the Nærøyfjord the vegetation changes from stands of lush, thermophilic deciduous trees, dry slopes in some of the lowest areas, barren and frost-exposed areas higher up in the mountains. A rare mutant variety of lime-tree with pale lemon-coloured leaves is found here and has been protected since 1933. The fauna is poor in species, but in the valleys there are relatively large concentrations of deer. The sea eagle, the golden eagle, the gyrfalcon, the white-backed woodpecker, and the snowy owl nest in this area, and there are also important summer biotopes for waders.

The old Royal Post Road along the Nærøyfjord from the farm, Styvi, is a beautiful cultural monument and it has become a popular road for hikers. When the official postal service was established in Norway in the 1640s, the post between Bergen and Oslo was transported by farmers by way of Voss down to Gudvangen. The post then went by boat on the Nærøyfjord and the Aurlandsfjord to Lærdal. The five-kilometre-long road was built because many a winter the ice in the inner part of the Nærøysfjord was thin and unsafe. From Styvi the post was taken across the fjord to Bakka on a so-called iceboat – a combination of boat and sledge. If the sledge broke through the ice, it functioned at once as a boat. From Bakka the post was carried to Gudvangen. In 1876, the steamship companies took over the postal service and they had their own travelling post offices onboard.

In the dramatic landscape along the Nærøyfjord just east of Styvi we find an incredible place called "Solaløysa" (literally: a place with no sun). This place just could not go by any other name, because regardless of the sun's position in the sky, the high mountains always block the sunrays from reaching down to this spot. However, the damp soil and the indirect heat from the mountainsides have made this place green and lush. High up in this narrow and precipitous landscape some people still eke out a living by keeping sheep and goats. Some of these farms are isolated, but people cling tenaciously to their way of life, and are determined to persevere however big the influence and the attractions are from the centralising market forces.

The small hamlet of Dyrdal is located on the Nærøyfjord. A short distance further west is the wooden church at Bakka, dating from 1859. In the 18th century Dyrdal was an administrative centre with a courthouse and an inn. In 1805, these two houses were moved to Gudvangen. Gradually, Gudvangen became built up with trade, transport, inn and later on hotel. The traffic increased with the construction of a road in the 1840s, which made it possible to drive by horse and cart between Voss and Gudvangen. The 1860s saw the first steamships and later on the big cruise liners. Before the First World War, close to 80 ships negotiated the narrow Nærøyfjord in the course of the summer season. An excursion to Stalheim by horse and chaise was a must, and this, of course, meant a lot of work – and money – for the local farmers.

Until November 2000, there was a regular ferry schedule on the Nærøyfjord linking Gudvangen, Kaupanger, and Lærdal. The same month the new tunnel between Aurland and Lærdal was opened for traffic, thus making the ferry superfluous. Now the ferries plying the Nærøyfjord in the summer season are marketed and run as a unique travel experience. The traffic increases from one year to the next and some 350,000 persons travel on these ferries every summer.

In 2005, the fjord landscape around the Nærøyfjord was inscribed on the prestigious UNESCO World Heritage List of the world's most unique natural and cultural monument sites worthy of preservation.

⏵The waterfall of Kjosfossen in Flåm cascades wildly down the mountainside.

Aurlandsfjorden.

THE FLÅM RAILWAY

The Flåm Railway is a branch line of the main Bergen Railway. The Bergen–Oslo Railway was completed in 1909, and the Flåm Railway was opened for traffic in 1940. This railway line has turned the village of Flåm into a major communication centre and tourist destination, and annually close to 500,000 travellers visit this place.

There are a number of reasons for this popularity: the Flåm Railway takes passengers from the fjord station of Flåm up to the mountain station of Myrdal 866 metres higher up. The scenery is unique and spectacular, and the technical solutions impressive. The tracks, the bends, and the tunnels constitute an ingenious construction feat – a manifestation of man's abilities to win over nature. At the same time, this stretch of railway line is a stubborn testimony of how it is possible to overcome political decisions and advice from so-called economic experts for nearly a century. In addition, this railway is an excellent example of how well things may go when local communities themselves can take control of infrastructure and communication facilities.

The great economic expansion of the Flåm Railway came after its privatization in 1994. The local council of Aurland and the savings bank of Aurland Sparebank were key contributors in securing local control of the Flåm Railway.

THE AURLANDSFJORD

On the west side of the Aurlandsfjord between the mountain of Beitelen and the village of Undredal is the mountain farm Stigen, 300 metres above sea level. On the eastern side of the fjord are the mountain farms of Horten and Nedberge offering a fantastic view. These farms are no longer in active use, but farmers from Undredal use the fields as pastures for their goats that are transported across the fjord in boats. The village of Undredal is an idyllic place. The place got a road connection only in the 1980s. Formerly people were completely dependent on passenger boats or their own smaller boats. In the dense settlement down by the quay lies the smallest church in the country, a weatherboard stave church dating from 1147 with a seating capacity for 40 persons only. This church also

At Myrdal railway station.

*The "Navvy road" is one of
Norway's best known bicycle tracks.*

served the whole Nærøyfjord area until the Bakka church was built in 1859.

Today Undredal is known for its goats and the production of genuine goat cheese. A new cheese factory has recently been built to compete with the big dairy companies. Two types of goat cheese – brown and white – are their main products. Demands for the brown goat cheese are actually bigger than the supply. Traditionally, the first weekend after the goats are taken up to the mountain pastures is an occasion for festivities, and, as a continuation of this tradition, a special goat-cheese festival is held in Undredal every year.

The Aurlandsdal valley is best known for its dramatic scenery, which impresses all hikers. There used to be several high farms in this valley, the highest of which was located at an altitude of 800 metres above sea level. They even had to have their own cemetery, because in wintertime it was too far and too dangerous to descend down to the Vangen church by the Aurlandsfjord.

FRØNNINGEN

At the entrance to the Aurlandsfjord lies Frønningen, a major forest-clad peninsula under the mountain of Blåskavlen. In the Norwegian society there was an ingrown scepticism to nobility and the upper class, and Frønningen is one of the few manors in the county. At this place we encounter the culture of the landowners from the 19th and 20th centuries.

Knut Rumohr (1916–2002), an artist of international repute, was born at this manor, and to this place he always returned. He decided early to become

On the manor of the Rumohr family at Frønningen lives Wilhelm Rumohr, son of the artist Knut Rumohr.

◁ Interior detail from the Frønningen residence.

an artist. The son of the landowner studied under Jean Heiberg and Georg Jacobsen at the Norwegian Academy of Arts in 1938. He soon made a name for himself as an accomplished printmaker, but it is above all as a painter that he is best known. His works of art became very much in demand both nationally and internationally. His roots go far back to the Norwegian rural culture. He had studied folk art since he was a teenager, and this study made an impression on him both as an artist and as a human being. He found his inspiration in nature, but he expressed it in a non-figurative style. In some of his paintings, he uses a violent brush, expressively and dramatically. His paintings are virtual explosions in red, black and dark blue with light effects in yellow and white.

Knut Rumohr was not only a full-blooded native of Sogn. He also lived for long periods in Oslo, and spoke two dialects. He used the Sogne dialect when in company with people from Sogn, but switched to the Bergen dialect when he spoke with other Norwegians. He had a deep respect for the culture of the people of Sogn. This is also shown in his collection activities. Surrounding a modern studio on his manor he has built up a rural museum with houses, objects and implements carefully restored by himself.

ÅRDAL – SOCIAL MODEL COMMUNITY

There are few places in our country where you get so close to our immediate and transformed past as in the street called "Statsråd Evensens veg" at

The industrial town of Øvre Årdal.

Årdals tangen. Now the street has become somewhat narrower than it used to. Previously it was oversized, reflecting the optimism and bright future prospects in the years after the Second World War. Lars Evensen was a sausage maker who became vice-president of the Norwegian Trade Union Congress, Minister of Trade (1945–1947), and Minister of Industry from 1947. As Minister of Trade and later Minister of Industry he played a key role in establishing industry in Årdal. He had an incredible capacity for work.

Årdal, the new and social model community, emerged from war remnants,

chaos and rust. The need for aluminium in the war industry formed the foundation for the industry. The war from 1940–45 saw the opening of the Flåm Railway and the Tyin hydroelectric power station. The post-war years gave us military machines, bulldozers and ballpoint pens for civilian use. Above all, the post-war years gave us Årdal which was the human dam that Sogn needed. Youths looking for work rushed to Årdal. They came straight from the sheep sheds in the neighbouring municipalities to become modern industrial shift workers. They became loyal members of trade unions and

⌁ In the western part of the Jotunheimen mountain massif there are lakes, summer pastures in the valleys as well as majestic peaks.

⌁ The hamlet of Indre Offerdal. The facility "Ne'fø sjøen" (literally: down by the seaside) from the transition period between the agrarian and the industrial communities.

the Norwegian Labour Party, which have always functioned as a protection wall for the Årdal community. Apart from one election, the Labour Party has been supported by 70% of the voters in Årdal ever since 1945.

Årdal is much more than a social model community. Årdal is also the gateway to the Jotunheimen Massif with its mountains and soaring peaks. This is where the Sognefjord meets the narrow valleys cutting into the moun-

tain massif with the impressive waterfall of Vettisfossen and the valley of Ut-
ladalen. The Sognefjord, the Jotunheimen Massif and the Vettisfossen waterfall cover everything that Norway has to offer its visitors.

THE LUSTRAFJORD

The trade capital of the Hansen family came to play a significant part for
Sogn. Jan Henrik had two sisters, Torborg and Susanna, who both married
captain Gerhard Munthe at Kroken. Through Gerhard Munthe, Sogn actu-

ally became a much-visited place for artists of national and international repute. Jan Henrik's mother, Mari, moved back to Luster and bought the Eide
farm at Skjolden. There she built a magnificent residence and an impressive
barn in stone. She got water from high up in the mountains and dug irriga-
tion ditches to lead the water out to the fields and pastures. Mari Eide died
in 1847, and her son-in-law captain Munthe took over the farm. However, he
had enough on his hands already, and in 1851, Steinar Torgeirson Sulheim
from the valley of Gudbrandsdalen became the owner of the farm. In this
way the Sulheim family entered the tourist business in Sogn. They became

famous mountain guides to the peaks of the western part of Jotunheimen, to the mountaintops of Fanaråken and Store Skagastølstind. The cradle of mountaineering, though, is found at Turtagrø. To sit there at the hotel and watch the mountains in all their splendour and majesty makes us feel grateful for what Mother Nature can give us. You yearn to use your feet to conquer new peaks. From Turtagrø it is possible to bike down to Øvre Årdal. You may ponder how the new Norway developed after the Second World War. The hydroelectric development in this, perhaps the finest countryside in Norway, created new workplaces in the industrial town of Årdal.

The municipality of Luster, with a land area that can match that of some of the eastern counties, is full of special cultural monuments and natural adventures. Luster is the village of Veitastrond known for its goat cheese, the lake of Hafslovatnet with its big trout, the ski centre at Heggmyrane, and not least, the picturesque fjord village of Solvorn. At Solvorn they have turned the old into something modern and new. Hotel Walaker has a special atmosphere with its profusion of flowers, its art exhibitions and an ideal setting by the dockside. In the summer months there is a ferry connection from Solvorn to Urnes and the Urnes stave church. You can also get to Urnes by driving around the whole Lustrafjord. "The romantic road" winds its way from Skjolden to Kinserdalen through a landscape of cascading waterfalls, where nearly every farm can be linked to characteristic features in our national history.

FROM FORTUN TO SYGNEFEST

There can be no doubt as to where the Sognefjord begins. This is out west by the ocean at Sygnefest or thereabouts. But where does the fjord end? Is it at Flåm, Lærdal or Årdalstangen? Many people have asked this question but it is hopeless to come up with a definite answer. On the other hand, it might be a good idea to stick to what in a national context, is held to be the end station of the fjord. It was Henrik Wergeland, our national poet, who defined where the fjord ends. "From Fortun to Sygnefest", he called the whole long area which is really the Sognefjord. The village of Fortun is located in the valley up from the head of the fjord east of Skjolden. The fact that the fjord "goes ashore" before ascending upwards towards the horizon is a good symbol of the diversity and the variations that the Sognefjord represents.

⊳ *The Urnes stavechurch at Ornes is the oldest preserved stave church in the country.*

MUNICIPALITIES

The facts are taken from Statistics Norway, The Norwegian Meteorological Institute and The Norwegian Forest and Landscape Institute
(22 February 2007).

	BERGEN	GULEN	SOLUND	HYLLESTAD	HØYANGER	BALESTRAND	VIK
Square kilometres	465,3	596	228	259	907	430	828
Population	242 158	2 417	877	1 502	4 448	1 406	2 847
Inhabitants per square kilometre	520	4	4	6	5	3	3
Administrative centre	Bergen	Eivindvik	Hardbakke	Hyllestad	Høyanger	Balestrand	Vikjaøyri
DISTRIBUTION OF AREA (%)							
Cultivated land, % (km²)	7 (33,7)	4 (19,2)	1,5 (3,5)	5 (13,6)	1,3 (11,6)	1,2 (5,0)	2,8 (23,3)
Forest, % (km²)	47 (220,2)	-	-	51 (131,4)	-	-	-
Lakes and rivers, % (km²)	4 (19,3)	4 (21,8)	4 (9,3)	4 (11,1)	6 (52,2)	4 (18,4)	4 (35,5)
CLIMATE							
Mean temperature January (in °C)	1	0,4	2,0	1,3	0,3	-0,6	-0,3
Mean temperature June (in °C)	12,7	11,8	11,3	12,2	13,3	13,7	13,5
Annual precipitation (in mm)	2105	3013	1874	2120	2436	1370	
EMPLOYMENT (%)							
Employment 16-74 years of age	70	74	71	71	74	74	76
Unemployed (16-74 of workforce)	3,7	2,2	3,0	1,7	1,4	0,9	1,7
Employment public management	29,3	33,7	41,6	38,9	35,0	47,6	33,7
Employment public and private sector	70,7	66,3	58,4	61,1	65,0	52,4	66,3
Primary industry	0,6	18,9	27,0	14,2	4,8	3,5	13,0
Secondary industry	18,3	21,1	14,4	25,5	41,8	19,6	26,8
Tertiary industry	81,1	60,0	58,6	60,3	53,4	76,9	60,2

	LEIKANGER	SOGNDAL	LÆRDAL	AURLAND	LUSTER	ÅRDAL
Square kilometres	185	745	1341	1488,7	2702,3	978,7
Population	2 199	6 836	2 155	1 733	4 889	5 549
Inhabitants per square kilometre	12	9	2	1	2	6
Administrative centre	Leikanger	Sogndal	Lærdal	Aurlandsvangen	Gaupne	Årdalstangen
DISTRIBUTION OF AREA (%)						
Cultivated land, % (km²)	2,3 (4,1)	3 (23,6)	0,9 (12,4)	0,5 (7,2)	1,4 (37,5)	0,1 (1,1)
Forest, % (km²)	-	36 (294,5)	-	-	-	-
Lakes and rivers, % (km²)	1 (2,6)	1 (9,6)	1 (16,7)	6 (84,8)	3 (69,6)	5 (45,7)
CLIMATE						
Mean temperature January (in °C)	-0,8	-2,4	-2,5	-4,0	-5,7	-3,0
Mean temperature June (in °C)	13,8	13,7	13,6	13,5	12,7	13,4
Annual precipitation (in mm)	979	1491	587	979	1174	870
EMPLOYMENT (%)						
Employment 16-74 years of age	77	77	75	74	73	70
Unemployed (16-74 of workforce)	1,3	1,5	1,1	2,0	1,9	1,5
Employment public management	55,9	31,4	47,0	39,5	38	26,4
Employment public and private sector	44,1	68,6	53,0	60,5	62	73,6
Primary industry	2,8	5,5	9,4	8,8	13,7	0,7
Secondary industry	25,3	18,9	14,1	17,6	22,4	51,9
Tertiary industry	71,9	75,6	76,4	73,6	63,9	47,4